Saving the Bees

A Nature On Our Doorstep Book

Annette Meredith

To the Birch Room,
Look after the bees!

Annette Meredith

For Austin and Nina

With thanks to my children
and to Ted for their ever-patient support and advice.

Saving the Bees

Part One – Nectar and Pollen

Did you ever stop to think about where honey comes from?

Honey comes from nectar, made by flowers and collected by bees.

Thousands of bees worked very hard to make this honey!

Nectar – a sugary liquid that plants make to attract bees, insects and birds.

Honey bees visit around two million flowers to make just one jar of honey. Honey tastes different depending on which flowers the bees have visited.

It takes twelve bees their whole lives to make one teaspoon of honey. Honey is very precious!

Hive – the name for the bees' home.

How do honey bees make honey? Each bee has a long tongue, called a proboscis, which acts like a straw as it sucks the nectar from the flowers. The bees eat some of the nectar, but they also have an extra stomach for carrying nectar called their honey stomach. It's like a bee-sized, built-in backpack, just for honey!

The honey stomach starts to turn the nectar into honey. When the bee has filled her honey stomach, she flies back to the hive and transfers the honey to the hive bees.

Bees collect pollen as well as nectar when they visit a flower.

Can you see the pollen these bees have collected on their legs?

The bee combs its fur with its front legs to gather the pollen and then presses it into an area with curved, stiff hairs on its back legs.

The areas that hold the pollen are called pollen baskets.

When the pollen baskets are full, they can hold as many as a million grains of pollen and the bee will have visited more than a thousand flowers.

This bee has filled her pollen baskets and will soon fly back to the hive. Pollen is an important food for bees.
Bees don't only collect pollen and nectar. They need water, not just to drink, but for cooling the hive.
They also collect a sticky sap from trees called propolis, sometimes called "bee glue", which they use in the hive.

Pollen is usually bright yellow, but it can also be pale, almost white. Pollen can even be unusual colors, like red and green.

Pollen is made up of tiny grains, often yellow, from the male part of a flower. It is very high in protein. This picture is of dried pollen, which some people like to add to their food.

Part Two – Life in the Hive

Here is a man-made hive. In the wild, it is often in a hollow tree.

Here are some of the bees at the entrance to the hive. Some are bringing in pollen, others are communicating with each other.

Guard bees make sure that only bees from their hive are allowed in.

Here are some honey bees inside a hive.

Cell – a small hexagonal compartment in a bee honeycomb.

To find the queen, look for green!

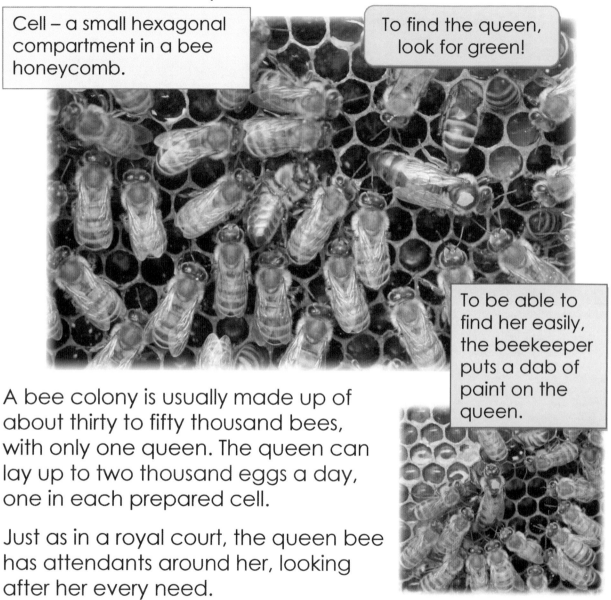

To be able to find her easily, the beekeeper puts a dab of paint on the queen.

A bee colony is usually made up of about thirty to fifty thousand bees, with only one queen. The queen can lay up to two thousand eggs a day, one in each prepared cell.

Just as in a royal court, the queen bee has attendants around her, looking after her every need.

Drones are bigger than worker bees

Worker bees are female and make up most of the bees in the hive.

A few of the bees in the hive are called drones. They are males and they don't work. They cannot sting and their only purpose in life is to mate with the queen.

Hexagons are one of only three shapes that can fit together without any gaps (can you name the other two?).
They make the hive very strong and they use the least amount of wax. Honeycomb has even been found in ancient tombs.

Larva – the tiny, wormlike form of a bee that emerges from an egg.

Beekeepers provide hives which have special parts called frames inside. This makes it easier for the bees to build their honeycomb cells made of wax. It's also easier for the beekeeper to collect the honey.

Look carefully, and you will see white larvae and sometimes a worker bee with its head in a cell feeding a larva. The larvae hatch from tiny eggs in the cells. The pupa is the next stage of the larva. It wraps itself in a cocoon and will emerge from its cell as a bee. From egg to worker bee takes about three weeks.

Most of the adults will be female worker bees and their first job will be to work in the hive.

1. The new worker bees will start by being cleaners, doing jobs like cleaning out cells ready for eggs, pollen or honey.

2. Next, they will become nurses, feeding and looking after the larvae. They will also remove any dead bees.

3. Then, some of the young bees will attend to the queen, in the royal court of the beehive!

4. Once the bees are about twelve days old, they can start producing wax and help to build the hive. They will also take honey and pollen from returning bees and help to regulate the temperature in the hive.

5. The last job before leaving the hive to forage for food is that of a guard, protecting the entrance to the hive.

6. Finally, after about three weeks, they will leave the hive to forage for nectar, pollen, water or propolis.

Bees usually fly up to about two miles from the hive in their search for nectar and pollen, but they may fly further.

Forage – to search over a wide area, usually for food.

Part Three – A Special Relationship

When you find a flower, you'll often find a bee as well. Sometimes, a bee has to climb right inside a flower to find nectar and pollen…

...sometimes, it just has to land on top!

Bees love flowers with open centers, like this coneflower. Flowers attract different kinds of pollinators, depending on their shape and color. Thin, tubular flowers are more attractive to hummingbirds and butterflies, which have long tongues so that they can reach deep inside the flowers.

Pollination – the transfer of pollen from the male part of the flower (the anther) to the female part (the stigma). This allows reproduction, which means the plant can make seeds which could grow into new plants.

When honey bees find a patch of flowers like this clover, they go back to the hive and do a special "bee dance", which tells the other bees where to go to find the flowers.

If the food source is close, they dance in a circle. If it's further away, they dance in a figure eight pattern known as a "waggle dance". They make a buzzing noise and waggle their bodies during part of the dance, which lets the other bees know in which direction and how far away the flowers are. They often use the sun to help guide them.

Making a beeline:
If you make a beeline for
something, you head straight for it!

Bees see colors differently from us. They can't see red, but they can see ultraviolet light, which makes this flower's colors look much darker on the landing area. It's like putting out a welcome mat!

UV Light - Violet is at one end of the color spectrum. Humans can't see UV light because it lies outside the visible spectrum of colors at the violet end. Bees can see UV light, and so can many other insects, birds and also some animals.

This bee has landed on a cosmos flower. The lines and darker color near the center guide the bee to the nectar and pollen.

Those two long feelers on the bee's head are called antennae. Each antenna can move in separate directions. They are used to touch, smell and taste.

Here you can see a bumblebee feeling and perhaps tasting the flower with its antennae.

Bees can smell scent in the air as they fly, helping them to find flowers more easily.

Can you find the proboscis, the antennae and the pollen baskets on this honey bee?

Bees are covered in tiny hairs. Pollen sticks to the hairs easily and is carried to other flowers. That's what the flowers want, so that they can be pollinated and produce seeds or fruits to make more plants. The bees and flowers help each other!

Bees and flowers have a symbiotic relationship.

The bees depend on the flowers for nectar and pollen.

The flowers depend on the bees to pollinate them.

Symbiosis – a relationship where both sides benefit.

This bee has a dusting of pollen on it from this passion flower. Do you see the stalk with the three branches on it, coming up from the middle of the flower? That is called the stigma, and if the bee brushes against it, the flower will be pollinated and can produce a fruit full of seeds that are able to make new plants.

This passion fruit grew from a passion flower because a pollinator visited the flower. A new plant may grow from the seeds in the fruit.

Part Four – Bees are Everywhere!

Without bees to pollinate them, many flowers, fruits and vegetables would not be able to reproduce. Fruits such as strawberries rely on bees to pollinate the flowers. Bees do a very important job.

Apple trees and many other trees also rely on bees to pollinate them.

There are more than 20,000 species of bee worldwide. About 4,000 species are found in America, most of them native bees. Every bee is a useful pollinator.

Let's take a look at some bees that aren't honey bees.

Striped abdomen

Not all bees live in hives. One of the bees on this sunflower is a bumblebee. It's easy to find, because it's so much bigger than the other two bees. The green bee with the long, striped abdomen is a different type of bee called a sweat bee.

There are a lot of different sweat bees. They are all small to medium-size bees that are mostly black or green in color and they can be so tiny that you can't even hear them buzz!

The tiny bee on this leaf is much smaller than in the picture.
It's only about the size of a fruit fly.
Without a magnifying lens, it's hard to tell that it's a bee.

Do you think this looks like a bee? Well, it is!

Sweat bees are very common, but not many people notice them because they are so small.

See if you can find one visiting a flower on a warm, sunny day!

Bumblebees live in smaller groups than honey bees, of only a few hundred rather than many thousands like the honey bees. They usually nest in the ground. Only the queens survive over the winter, and they build a new nest in the spring.

Many native bees, for example the mason bee, nest in tubes. These could be hollow reeds, canes or holes in wood made by wood-boring insects. Mason bees are sometimes called orchard bees, because they are so good at pollinating fruit trees.

Part Five – Be Nice to Bees

If there were no bees and we lost the plants that bees pollinate, it would affect not only people but also the ecosystem, or all living things. That's why we have to do everything we can to help the bees.

Looking after the environment is an important way to make sure that there will always be bees and other pollinators.

Ecosystem - A community of living and non-living things (water, soil, air, plants and everything living) that work together to create a balance. It can be big or small.

One easy way to help the bees is to grow flowers, especially ones they like. The birds and butterflies love flowers, too!

Bees love native wildflowers like this jewelweed.

Bees are attracted to flowers in shades of purple and violet, like this lavender.

Brightly colored flowers like the yellow sunflower are always very popular too.

See if you can find out which flowers the bees like best in your back yard!

This honey bee is busy collecting pollen from a sunflower. Its hairs have pollen stuck to them. That pollen will brush against the stigmas of other sunflowers as the bee visits them all.

Here is a goldfinch enjoying a sunflower seed.
Without insects like bees to pollinate it, this sunflower might not have produced seeds.
Seeds are a very important food for many different birds.
We are not the only ones to depend on bees - many other creatures depend on bees, too.

We should try to avoid spraying plants with pesticides. Pesticides kill bees and other insects like butterflies and ladybugs, not just the pests they are meant to kill.

Most insects are beneficial, meaning that they help us. Insects are also an important food for creatures like birds and small mammals.

Pesticide – A chemical substance or mixture that is designed to kill pests, but may also poison or kill other creatures.

All through the summer and into fall, bees are visiting flowers to collect nectar to make into honey so that they can survive the winter, when not many flowers are blooming and bees need to stay in the hive for warmth. They make more honey than they need, but we must always leave plenty for them.

Although most people think of the honey bee when a bee is mentioned, native bees are just as important as honey bees and just as good at pollinating. They have been part of the ecosystem in America for much longer than honey bees, which were brought here by the early European settlers.

The honey bee is the only insect that produces a food that people eat too. Many hives produce between fifty and a hundred pounds of honey that the bees don't need.
The beekeeper takes the frames out of the hive and scrapes the wax caps off the honeycomb. Then the frames are put in a centrifuge, which is a machine that spins the frames and forces the honey to come out of the comb.

Have you ever tried clover honey, or heather honey, or orange blossom honey? What's your favorite honey?

Honey has been used since ancient times to treat burns and help prevent infection.

Honey bees give us more than just honey. They also give us beeswax, pollen and propolis. Beeswax is good for making things like candles, soaps, creams and lotions. Pollen and propolis are sometimes used in medicines, and so is honey.

Perhaps you've drunk hot honey and lemon, or sucked a honey lozenge, to make your sore throat feel better?

Some people believe that if they eat honey or pollen from bees that have collected nectar from local flowers, it will help to prevent pollen allergies.

Although a lot of bees are able to sting, they'd rather not and they won't unless they think they are in danger. They are peaceful creatures and spend their days being very busy, working together to look after all the family of bees in the hive. Have you heard the expression "as busy as a bee"? Well, it's true!

The world would be a very different place without bees and we must do all we can to save and protect them.

Next time you see a flower, look for a busy bee!

Bee house project

Mason (or orchard) bees are native bees that are great pollinators, especially for fruit trees.
They are very gentle, solitary bees that like to nest separately but in small groups. You can buy mason bee houses, or make your own – it's easy!

Roll some paper around a pencil at least three times and secure it with sticky tape. Pull out the pencil and close one end with tape, or press one end into damp mud and let it dry. Make as many tubes as you like. The tubes should be between four and eight inches long. Pack them in a box or larger tube, open end facing out.

Protect them from the rain and hang the collection of tubes on an east or south-facing tree or wall in a quiet, sheltered area, at least three feet from the ground. The bees nest in spring and the young will emerge the following spring.

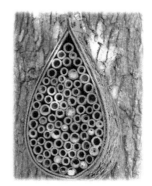

There are lots of different ways to make your bee house or hotel. "Bee" creative!

snapdragon

Remember to plant flowers for the bees!
Butterflies and hummingbirds love the flowers too!

Bees love these flowers!

nasturtium

Tall verbena

What else can we do to help the bees?

Plant flowers and herbs

Bee balm and black-eyed Susan

Bees prefer native species, so let wildflowers grow, or plant some. Leave those dandelions or that patch of clover in your lawn. Try to resist spraying with pesticides. Remember that most bugs are beneficial or benign – some estimates say as many as 99% – and pesticides don't discriminate.

Human-induced habitat loss affects every living thing and gardeners now have an important role in preserving habitat and protecting wildflower species. Aim to have a succession of blooms throughout the year. Most flowers are easy to grow; even if you only plant one flower, you will be helping the entire ecosystem.

Plant any of these, and you'll be the "bee's knees"!

Lavender	Sunflower	Clover	Cosmos
Nasturtium	Catnip	Bee Balm	Verbena
Snapdragon	Rosemary	Thyme	Aster

lavender

Make a Bee Bath

Bees also need water!
A bird bath may be too deep for them, so line a shallow dish with a few stones, which act as landing pads so that they can safely drink the fresh water. Having a muddy patch is also useful for solitary bees, as they use mud in home construction.

Speak up for the bees

Bees do not attack, they only defend. Many bees don't sting at all and the ones that can will only sting when provoked.

 Bee populations are declining at an alarming rate. Various studies have pointed to many possible reasons: climate change (colder winters); loss of habitat and reduced biodiversity as a result of human intervention; vast monocultures; parasitic mites and disease; the rampant use of pesticides and herbicides. As well as many native wildflowers being under threat, big home improvement stores and garden centers are often stocked with plants that have been treated with neonicotinoids, a group of pesticides that are deadly to bees.

Bees are a vital part of the ecosystem and their value to the US economy alone is estimated at between $15 and $20 billion a year. Look for on-line petitions and other initiatives by environmental groups to bring the bees' plight to the attention of state and federal government.

Vote with your wallet by buying local and organic food if possible. Ask if a plant has been treated with pesticides before buying it. Retailers will respond to consumer choice. Farmers will respond to demand for organic and non-GMO.

Bees are fascinating creatures that have been around longer than humankind. We need them much more than they need us.

ABOUT THE AUTHOR

Annette Meredith is a master gardener, photographer and lifelong student of nature who is passionate about environmental issues and conservation. She was born in England but now lives in North Carolina, where she enjoys encouraging, observing and photographing nature as she works to improve sixty acres of woodland, meadows and organic gardens.

Made in the USA
Charleston, SC
12 March 2015